## Just the Facts

# Genetic Engineering

### Steve Parker

# www.heinemann.co.uk/library

Visit our website to find out more information about **Heinemann Library** books.

To order:

 Phone 44 (0) 1865 888066

 Send a fax to 44 (0) 1865 314091

Visit the Heinemann Bookshop at www.heinemann.co.uk/library to browse our catalogue and order online.

**Produced by Monkey Puzzle Media Ltd**
Gissing's Farm, Fressingfield, Suffolk IP21 5SH, UK

First published in Great Britain by Heinemann Library, Halley Court, Jordan Hill, Oxford OX2 8EJ, part of Harcourt Education.
Heinemann is a registered trademark of Harcourt Education Ltd.

Editorial: Clare Weaver, Sarah Eason and
  Louise Galpine
Design: Mayer Media Ltd
Picture Research: Lynda Lines and Frances Bailey
Consultant: Nick Thomson
Production: Camilla Smith

Originated by Ambassador Litho Ltd
Printed and bound in Hong Kong, China by
  South China Printing Company

ISBN 0 431 16178 X
09 08 07 06 05
10 9 8 7 6 5 4 3 2 1

**British Library Cataloguing in Publication Data**
Parker, Steve
Genetic Engineering
660.6'5
A full catalogue record for this book is available from the British Library.

**Acknowledgements**
The publishers would like to thank the following for permission to reproduce photographs:
Art Archive p. **9 top** (Archaeological Museum, Baghdad/Dagli Orti); Associated Press pp. **33** (Henry Salim), **48** (Joe Cavaretta); Alamy pp. **5 top** (Janine Weidel), **43** (Sue Cunningham/ World Wide Pictures Agency); Corbis pp. **5 bottom** (Charles O'Rear), **16** (Sygma), **21** (Ron Sanford), **25** (Dennis Wilson), **30** (Jonathan Blair), **36** (Michael Callan/FLPA); Panos Pictures p. **40** (David Dahmen); Rex Features pp. **6** (Phanie Agency), **10 main image** (SFT), **10 inset** (Florence Durand/SIPA), **12** (UTN), **45** (Assignments Photographers); Robert Harding Picture Library **34**; Roslin Institute **31**; Science Photo Library pp. **14** (Geoff Tomkinson), **15** (A B Dowsett), **17** (Vittorio Luzzati), **18** (NIBSC), **23** (Simon Fraser), **24** (Mauro Fermariello), **26** (Edelmann), **37** (M H Sharp), **42** (Dr Yorgas Nikas); Still Pictures p. **38** (Sean Sprague); Topham Picturepoint pp. **9 main image** (Pressnet), **28** (Josef Polleross/Image Works), **47** (Dion Ogust).

Cover photograph reproduced with permission of Alamy (Ed Kashi/Phototake Inc).

Every effort has been made to contact copyright holders of any material reproduced in this book. Any omissions will be rectified in subsequent printings if notice is given to the publishers.

Any words appearing in the text in bold, **like this**, are explained in the Glossary.

# Contents

# Introduction

Many people are familiar with the amazing progress of computers and the Internet. But how many know about another area of science and technology, advancing at a similar rate? Important discoveries are made almost weekly in the field of **genetics**. But what does the science of genetics involve? What are **genes**, and how are they engineered?

## The genetic material

Genes are chemical substances. They are made of the chemical known as **DNA**, de-oxyribonucleic acid, sometimes called 'the genetic material'. DNA is so small that it is difficult to imagine its size. The amount of DNA in a typical plant or animal, is far too small to see under an ordinary microscope. Millions of genes would require an amount of DNA only the size of the dot on this 'i'.

Genes are also instructions. Like the list of tasks in an instruction book, genes carry information. Genetic information controls how living things grow, develop, carry out life processes and survive. Every living thing or organism, from the tiniest germ to the biggest animal or tree, has its own set of genes. These are the detailed instructions, in the form of DNA, for how it lives and grows.

## Engineering new life

Engineers are people who design and build new machines and structures, from great bridges and trucks to tiny electronic devices. **Genetic engineering** or GE is sometimes also known as genetic modification or GM. It happens when genes are moved or transferred from one kind of living thing into another kind where they would not naturally occur.

The transfer of genes is usually carried out by scientists in the laboratory. The new combinations of genes 'built' by genetic engineers result in new versions of living things, which would not otherwise occur in nature. The new combinations can also create man-made or synthetic forms of life.

# Similar but different

Between one living thing and another, genes are not all completely different. In many living things, some of the genes are exactly the same, while others are very similar. The similarity between genes in different forms of life is one reason why genetic engineering is possible. When genes from one kind of living thing are put into another kind, their instructions may be carried out – or they may not. As this book shows, the process is long and complicated and subject to chance.

There are more than 6000 million people in the world. Each of us has a unique individual appearance, largely due to the genes we inherit.

**❝The three great themes in 20th-century science are the atom, the computer and the gene.❞**

Results of the Millennium Science Survey 2000, in which people worldwide voted on the Internet for the most important three areas of scientific progress during the preceding century

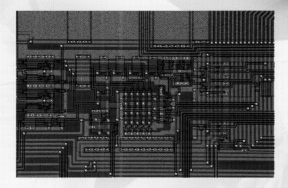

Computer microchips (electronic circuits) contain thousands of complex microscopic parts. Yet a living thing's genes are even smaller and more complex.

# Genes and inheritance

Eye colour is just one of the thousands of bodily features controlled by genes inherited from a person's parents.

Genes are more than the instructions setting out how individual living things develop and survive. They are also vital in how living things breed or reproduce. When parents reproduce, they pass on their genes to the offspring. These offspring grow and develop according to the instructions in the genes they received, or **inherited**, from their parents. This is why offspring are similar to their parents. The inheritance of genes is the reason why living things breed to produce more of their own kind, rather than producing other kinds of living things.

## What genes do

A single gene can be imagined as an instruction to make one part of a living thing. The part may be large, like a whole limb or wing. Or it may be tiny, such as a certain chemical involved in digesting food. An example is the gene for eye colour in humans. It contains the instructions for how to make the pigment (coloured substance) in the ring-shaped part of the eye, the iris. There are several versions of this gene. One version has the instructions for making a blue pigment. Another version is for brown pigment, another for green, and so on. So the colour of a person's eyes depends on the genes inherited from her or his parents.

## Genes together

Many thousands of genes control the size, shape and structure of the human body's many parts, as well as the way these parts work to carry out life processes. Also, individual genes rarely work alone. Some body parts are controlled by two, three, four or more genes, all working closely together. Throughout a single living thing, thousands of genes work together, interact and affect each other.

## Genes and environment

A living thing does not grow and survive according to its genes alone. There are many other influences on its development and survival. They include the food and nutrients it obtains (or lack of them), injuries, disease, weather conditions such as severe cold or a sudden dry spell, and many similar events. So each living thing is partly the result of its genes, and partly the result of its life history and its surroundings or **environment**.

# What genes are made of

In most living things, **genes** are made of a chemical substance known as **DNA**, de-oxyribonucleic acid. DNA is very tiny but also very complicated. It has a special shape called a **double helix**, which looks like the two sides of a long ladder, twisted like corkscrews. The width of DNA is just two **nanometres**. Enlarged about one million times, it would be as wide as this letter 'l'.

## Cells and chromosomes

Living things are made of **microscopic** building blocks called **cells**. These vary in size and shape but, on average, about 40–50 of them lined up in a row would stretch across this full stop. The human body consists of more than 50,000,000,000,000 cells (50 million million). The DNA that makes up genes is found inside the cell's blob-like control centre, known as the **nucleus**.

The full set of DNA in the nucleus is in 46 separate lengths, which are called **chromosomes**. The DNA of each chromosome is coiled and looped like a wound-up rope to make it much shorter. Stretched out, the longest piece of human DNA, which is in chromosome 1, would be more than 70 millimetres long. Coiled up, it is thousands of times shorter. Along with all the other chromosomes, it fits easily inside the cell's nucleus. The full set of DNA for all the genes is found in each cell.

## The genetic code

DNA is like a twisted ladder. The 'rungs' of the ladder are pairs of chemical sub-units known as **bases**. There are four different bases, called A (adenine), T (thymine), G (guanine) and C (cytosine). These bases make up, in chemical form, a very short four-letter code. In different combinations or sequences they 'spell out' instructions for the cell to use during its life processes. The order of the bases in a particular section of DNA is a chemical code. It tells the cell to make a certain product – that is, the bases form a gene.

In a living thing, cells multiply to produce more cells. This happens so that the whole organism can grow, and to replace old cells that die as part of natural life processes. Each time a cell multiplies, it copies its whole set of DNA, so that all the genes are passed on. This means every individual cell in a living thing contains the full set of DNA, representing all the genes.

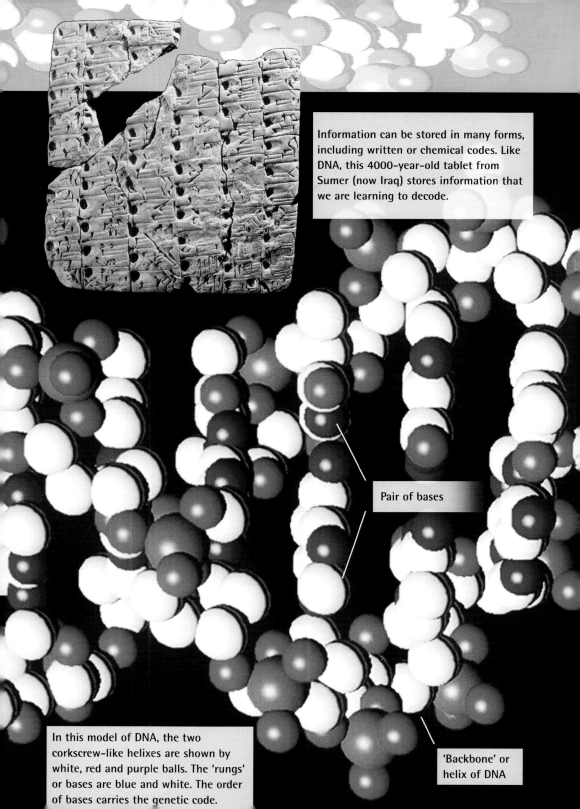

Information can be stored in many forms, including written or chemical codes. Like DNA, this 4000-year-old tablet from Sumer (now Iraq) stores information that we are learning to decode.

Pair of bases

In this model of DNA, the two corkscrew-like helixes are shown by white, red and purple balls. The 'rungs' or bases are blue and white. The order of bases carries the genetic code.

'Backbone' or helix of DNA

# Genetic variety and genomes

The full set of **genes** in a living thing is called its **genome**. The total number of genes varies from just a few hundred in **microscopic** germs, to many thousands in animals and plants. A tiny worm called *Caenorhabditis* has about 18,000 genes, while a human being has an estimated 30,000 – 35,000. The complete sequence of all the sub-units or **bases** in the human genome was worked out in the year 2000. However, the exact identity of all the genes, how they work and what they produce, will take many more years to discover.

## Different genes

As explained earlier, most genes exist in several versions. In human beings, the gene for eye colour may be brown, blue, grey, green and so on. In a tree, the gene for leaf shape might be for a long, slim leaf or a shorter, wider one. The difference between these versions of the

ATGCTGCCGATTTAAAGCGCGTATTTCAGATTATGCGGACAGAT
AGACATAGGACAGATACAGATTTAAAGCGCGTCAGATTCAGAT
TTAAGCGCGTAGACATAGGACATATGCGACATAGGGGACAGATA
GTACAGATTATGCTGCCGATCCAGATTATGCTGCCGATCAGAT
CAGATTATGCATGCTGCCGATTTATGCTTAAAGCGCGACATAGG
TAAAGCGCGTCAGATTATGCCTTAAAGCGCCCCGTAGACATAG
AGATTATGCAAGCGCGTAGACGGACAGATACAGATTATGCTGCC
GTTAAAGCGCGATACAGATTATGATTCAGATTATGCAGACCGACA
AGACATTTTAGGACAGATACAGGCGCGTAGACATTAAAGCGCGT
ATTTCAGATTATGCGGACAGATAGACATAGGACATGCTGCCGAT
TTAAAGCGCGTCAGATTCAGATATGCTGCCGATTTAAAGCGCGT
TATGCGACATAGGGGACAGATAAGACATAGGCAGATACAGATT
CAGATTATGCTGCCGATCAGATTTAAGCGCGTAGACATAGGACA
TATGCTTAAAGCGCGACATAGGGATACAGATTATGCTGCCGATC
TTAAAGCGCCCCGTAGACATAGCAGATTATGCATGCTGCCGATT
GACAGATACAGATTATGCTGCCTAAAGCGCGTCAGATTATGCC
GATTCAGATTATGCAGACGACAAGATTATGCAAGCGCGTAGACG
GCGCGTAGACATTAAAGCGCGTGTTAAAGCGCGATACAGATTAT
AGACATAGGACATGCTGCCGATAGACATTTTAGGACAGATACAG

This is just a tiny section of the information in the human genome. The letters represent the four bases in DNA (see page 8). The whole genome is four million times longer.

10

same genes, and between the different kinds of genes in different living things, is known as genetic variety or variation.

In general, genetic variety is very small between different individuals of the same kind of living thing, such as the different people who make up the human species. We have about 999 out of every 1000 genes the same as each other. The variety becomes

greater between similar kinds or species of living things, such as between humans, chimpanzees and gorillas. Even so, in humans and chimps, on average, 99 out of every 100 genes are the same. Between very different kinds of living things, the variety in genes becomes greater. Between a mouse and a mushroom, for example, about 40 out of every 100 genes are the same.

## The human genome

- The complete human genome has all the genetic instructions needed for the human body to develop and run itself.

- The genes are in the form of 23 pairs of **chromosomes**, seen under a powerful microscope as X-like shapes inside the **nucleus** of each single **cell**.

- Humans have between 30,000 and 35,000 genes in total.

- The complete number of sub-units or bases (A, C, T and G) in DNA is 3,164,700,000 (just over 3000 million, or 3 billion).

- If all the DNA in all the chromosomes from one cell was uncoiled, stretched straight and joined end-to-end, its total length would be about 2 metres.

Human beings and chimpanzees may look different, but more than 99 out of every 100 genes are the same in these two kinds, or species, of living things.

# Changing genes

Genes can change or mutate at any time. This squirrel had normal-looking parents, but there has been a mutation in its gene for making the brown colour in its fur and eyes.

**Genes** do not stay the same for ever. Inside a living thing, **cells** are continually multiplying, both for growth and repair, and to replace old, worn-out cells. As a cell multiplies, it copies lengths of its **DNA** to pass to its two offspring cells. But sometimes alterations or changes happen in the copying, which are known as **mutations**. These may or may not affect the way the gene works. If they do, it may be beneficial to the living thing. For example, one type of mutation may give an animal more powerful muscles for faster running. Another type of mutation may be harmful, perhaps causing the muscles to be weaker. Some mutations produce no effects on the living thing and are known as neutral.

Similarly, when living things breed or reproduce, genes are passed as the DNA in the egg and sperm cells, from parents to offspring. Mutations may also occur when this DNA is copied. So the offspring **inherit** the mutated gene. Again, the effects may be either beneficial, harmful or neutral.

## New combinations

Genes can change in other ways too. Sometimes when cells multiply, as described above, pieces of **chromosomes** carrying dozens or hundreds of genes become detached and then join to different chromosomes. This 'crossing over' results in new collections or groups of genes, known as **recombination**.

Both mutation and recombination are natural processes and produce continuing genetic variety. This is why offspring are usually similar to, but not exactly the same as, their parents. They have slightly different versions and combinations of genes from their parents. (An exception to this is when individuals have exactly the same genes as each other, as happens with identical twins. This is described on page 30.)

## Breaking down barriers

In nature, mutations, recombinations and other forms of genetic variation usually occur only within the same species of living thing. This is because individual living things only breed naturally with others of their own species (or very rarely, with members of very similar species). So, mutated genes and new gene combinations can occur in one species, but cannot transfer or cross from one species to another. One of the major features of **genetic engineering** is that it can break through this 'species barrier'. It can transfer genes from one kind of living thing to a very different kind.

# GE techniques

Genetic engineering alters **genes** and transfers or moves them between living things, using laboratory processes and equipment. The exact techniques vary, but the general method is to use **microscopic** living things called viruses or **bacteria**. Some of these reproduce naturally by moving their own genes into other living things, to make these other living things produce copies of the viruses or bacteria. Scientists adapt the process so that the microbes move different genes – the 'desired' genes, with the instructions for a new feature, which they wish to transfer.

## Extracting the genes

Genetic scientists take out or extract the genetic material, **DNA**, from **cells** of the **donor** living thing – the one with the 'desired' gene. The DNA is split by chemicals known as **restriction enzymes**, into smaller lengths or sequences. These are tested to find the ones that carry the required gene. These pieces are then added to the viruses, which will work as 'carriers' for the gene. Especially useful are the types of viruses known as **phages**. Alternative carriers are ring-shaped pieces of DNA known as plasmids. For GM crops, certain types of bacteria found naturally in the soil are used as carriers.

The laboratory technique called gel electrophoresis separates various pieces of DNA as dark bars. The order and spacing of the 'bar code' reveals the genetic information.

The 'carriers' are added to **recipient cells** – those intended to take up the genes. The 'carriers' add their own genetic material and the extra gene into the recipient cells. The cells are tested to see if the transferred gene has become part of their genetic material. If the transfer is successful these cells begin to use the instructions in the new gene, to produce the desired product.

The recipient cells may be growing in a laboratory. Or they may be inside a whole living thing or organism, which is now known as a **genetically engineered** or genetically modified organism (GEO or GMO). The genetic material, DNA, has been put together in new selections or combinations, using transferred genes. It is called recombinant or transgenic DNA.

## Down to chance

Genetic techniques are by no means reliable. It may take hundreds or thousands of attempts to transfer a gene, or it may never work at all. Each living thing is like a hugely delicate and complex machine, and altering or swapping its parts is very tricky. Imagine taking a microchip out of one computer and inserting it into another, very different kind of computer, without the full instructions. The chances of it working are slim.

A plasmid is a loop of genetic material – DNA. Scientists can put an extra gene or piece of DNA into it, and then use the plasmid to add the new gene into a living thing.

**15**

# An age-old process

A form of **genetic engineering** has been going on for thousands of years. This is **selective breeding** or artificial selection, when people select or choose which living things to breed together. The living things are chosen because of certain features, such as plenty of meat on an animal, or large fruits on a plant. People have used selective breeding gradually to alter the genetic make-up of living things. From wild ancestors they have produced domesticated farm animals such as goats, sheep, pigs, horses and cows, and pets such as dogs and cats. Farm plants, such as wheat, rye, barley, rice and other crops, and various kinds of flowers and trees in horticulture, have also been created.

## Limits of selective breeding

Selective breeding can only use **genes** that occur in nature. It can only be carried out within a species. The process usually takes many generations, perhaps hundreds of years. Modern genetic engineering can make new kinds of genes,

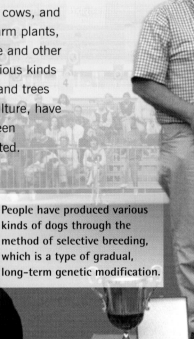

People have produced various kinds of dogs through the method of selective breeding, which is a type of gradual, long-term genetic modification.

16

transfer them between species, and do this in one or two generations.

## Genetics as a science

The science of **genetics** began in the 1850s. Austrian monk Gregor Mendel carried out experiments on garden peas, selectively breeding generations of different sizes and colours. Mendel worked out the basic laws of heredity and suggested it was due to 'particles' of inheritance, which we now call genes.

A century later in Cambridge, UK, James Watson and Francis Crick worked out the shape of **DNA**. The **double helix** shape showed how genes could copy themselves, and DNA became known as the 'molecule of life'. In the 1960s the genetic code was worked out, showing which DNA **bases** were the instructions for which products. The 1970s saw the early attempts to move genes artificially from one living thing to another.

## Helpful pictures

To work out the shape of DNA, Watson and Crick used information in pictures produced by another scientist, Rosalind Franklin, in London. She used the invisible rays called X-rays (similar to those used in medicine) to make the images. Franklin was the first person to make such images and they were vital in the discovery of DNA's double helix structure. However, Franklin never received full credit for her contribution, while Watson and Crick, along with Franklin's colleague Maurice Wilkins, received a Nobel Prize in 1962.

Rosalind Franklin (1920–58) made X-ray pictures of DNA crystals, which Watson and Crick used to discover its detailed structure.

# GE and biotechnology

From the 1980s, scientists began to improve the methods of **genetic engineering** or modification, especially transferring **genes** into the microbes known as **bacteria** (as described on the previous pages). This area of science has become known as **biotechnology** – using microbes and other organisms as 'living machines' or 'living factories' to make products, by putting genes into them from other, different organisms.

## Beer and bread

Some forms of biotechnology have been in use for centuries. The microbes called yeast use sugar as an energy source and make what is, for them, a waste substance – alcohol. People have long used yeasts to make alcoholic drinks such as beers and wines. Similarly, yeasts have been used to make bread 'rise' by producing tiny bubbles of gas as it is baked. However, in these traditional methods, the types or strains of yeast had to be selected from those available in nature. Using modern GM methods, new strains of yeast can be made almost 'to order'.

## Saving suffering and lives

One of modern biotechnology's first successes, in the early 1980s, was using microbes as 'living factories' to make the substance **insulin**. This is a natural body substance called a **hormone**, and it controls the body's use of energy. Some people suffer from

These coloured 'rods' are bacterial microbes known as *E. coli*, magnified about 4000 times. Extra genes are put into *E. coli* to make it produce useful substances such as medical drugs.

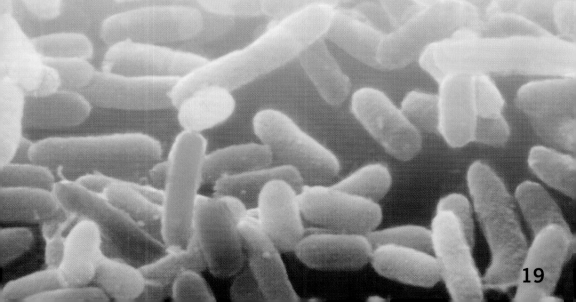

diabetes, where the body cannot make enough insulin. Untreated, it can cause illness and possibly death. The gene with the instructions for making insulin was added to the microbes, which then became 'living factories' that could make insulin. Before this, people with diabetes used animal insulin, purified from cows or pigs. This was similar to human insulin, but not exactly the same. The engineered microbes made human insulin, which was much more suitable for many people with diabetes.

Similar work has been done with other substances for medical treatment. They include clotting factor, given to people with haemophilia, where the blood does not clot properly in a wound or cut. Other successful biotechnology products include various **antibiotic** drugs, which fight infection by bacterial microbes. As more microbes become resistant to (unharmed by) existing antibiotics, GM bacteria that make new antibiotics may become especially valuable in the future. Another product is **interferon**, which is used against viruses and some forms of **cancer**.

## PCR

One of the most important techniques in genetic engineering is PCR, polymerase chain reaction. This was devised in the late 1980s and is used to copy lengths of **DNA** quickly and efficiently in the laboratory. Modern versions of PCR are central in much genetic work.

# GM crops

GM or genetically modified crops were first tested in small-scale trials in 1986, and grown on a large or commercial (money-making) scale in 1996 in the USA. Around the world, dozens of crops are being **genetically engineered** to give them new features. However, it is a long and complex process from the first tests on GM plants in a laboratory, to full-scale production in huge fields (see page 21).

## Why are crops modified?

There are several reasons for genetically modifying farm crops. The main one at present is for increased resistance to sprayed chemicals. These include herbicides or weedkillers, which kill off weeds growing among the crop, and pesticides, which remove small animals such as insects and worms. The genetically modified crops will be less affected by these chemical sprays.

Another reason to modify crops is to gain increased yields, such as bigger grains in cereal crops like wheat. Further aims are to make the products last longer and stay in better condition as they are harvested, transported and put on store shelves, and to produce crops with increased amounts of nutrients such as vitamins, like 'Golden Rice' (see page 41).

## A strange case

One of the 'Top Ten' crops undergoing genetic modification is tobacco. This may seem odd, when smoking tobacco is known to cause immense suffering and millions of deaths around the world. To anti-smoking campaigners, a complete ban on tobacco might be more appropriate. However, the tobacco industry employs millions of people, and growing this crop earns money for farmers in many poor regions. Some genetic development is aimed at reducing the levels of dangerous substances in this plant, which could make smoking less harmful.

Many weedkillers sprayed on to crops also affect the crop to some extent, perhaps by slowing its growth. Crops can be changed genetically so they are not harmed by the weedkiller, which still removes the weeds.

## Testing a GM crop

1 The new crop is first grown under carefully controlled laboratory conditions, where its pollen or seeds or other parts cannot leave the test site. This not only prevents loss or 'escape' of genetic material, it also protects workers from the possibly harmful effects of these new life-forms.

2 The numbers of specimens are increased, for example, by growing a crop in small, self-contained greenhouses and glasshouses.

3 Next come limited field trials in the countryside. The crop is grown in small plots carefully chosen with 'buffer zones' around to minimize gene spread and risks to the environment.

4 Pre-production or farm-scale trials occur, covering large fields. Crops and wildlife around are tested to see if the gene is 'escaping'.

5 If all these stages are satisfactory, full commercial production may begin.

# GM animals

More than 200 different kinds of animals have now been altered by **genetic engineering**, including pigs, cows, sheep, rats, mice, and fish such as salmon and trout. As in plants, there are several reasons for genetic modification. They include faster growth and a larger size when adult. This means we get more of the animal's products, and we get them faster. For example, GM 'supersalmon' grow more than twice as fast as normal, non-GM salmon. Some modification is for increased yields of the animal products we use, such as more milk from cows and leaner (less fatty) meat in pigs.

More specialist examples of genetic modification include animals such as sheep, which have been engineered to produce medical products such as **antibiotic** drugs. The **gene** is taken from the living thing in which this product was originally found – for an antibiotic drug, this could be a mould or fungus. (The first antibiotic drug, penicillin, was so named because it was discovered in a mould, *Penicillium*.) The gene for making the drug is isolated and put into the animal, with the aim that the animal produces the drug in its milk. The drug can then be purified from the milk and used to treat patients.

GM mice and rats have been produced for use in the laboratory, for example, to test new medical drugs.

As with plant crops, it is a long and complex process from the first production and tests of GM animals, to rearing them on a commercial or money-making scale. In some cases the animals grow well at first, but then develop disabilities or diseases. Latest estimates predict that very few kinds of GM animals being tested today, perhaps fewer than one in 100, will eventually become successful on a large scale.

## GM pets

Not all GM animals are being reared for us to eat or use their products. GM is also being used in the pet trade. Some jellyfish and other creatures naturally glow at night in the dark ocean. The genes that have the instructions for their glow-in-the-dark substances have been put into fish, frogs and even mice and rabbits, so that they glow too. Several new kinds of fish have already been bred in this way for the aquarium trade.

'Super-salmon' grow twice as fast as ordinary ones. If they are reared in huge sea cages, and then escape, they could spread their genes to wild salmon.

# Genetic conditions in people

Genetic conditions are those that are due to abnormal or faulty **genes**. In some cases the abnormal genes are **inherited** from parents. However, the way genes work means that the parents may not have the same condition, and may have no reason to suspect that they have any abnormal genes at all. In other cases, the abnormal genes are not inherited but appear in the body as it grows and develops. This may happen in the early stages of life, as a foetus grows in the womb. Genes can be altered by various causes, including harmful **radiation** or radioactivity and certain chemicals or drugs.

In cystic fibrosis, the breathing airways and lungs clog with mucus (thick fluid). Tapping the chest loosens the mucus so it can be coughed up.

## The range of genetic conditions

About one baby in eighty is born with a genetic condition that requires medical treatment. (However this proportion varies greatly in different regions around the world.) Some of the better-known genetic conditions include:

- Haemophilia, in which blood does not clot properly to seal a wound

- Cystic fibrosis, which alters the workings of the lungs and affects breathing

- Sickle cell disorder, when the blood cannot carry oxygen effectively

- Spina bifida, where the spinal cord and spinal bones (backbone) do not form properly.

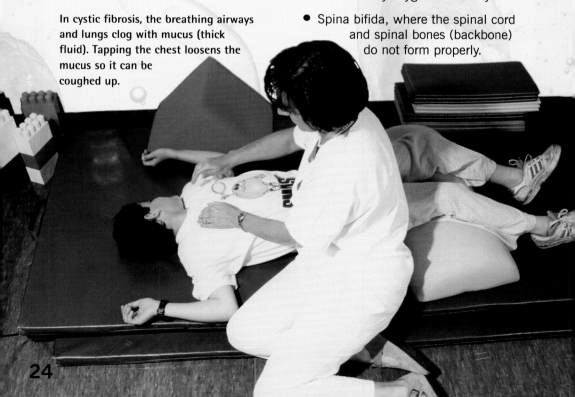

About 500 genetic conditions occur fairly frequently. There are also many thousands of much rarer ones, where there are only a few new cases around the world each year. And, due to the continuing process of **mutation** (see page 13), occasionally genetic conditions appear which are new – they have never been seen or studied before.

## One gene or more?

In some cases, a genetic condition is due to a single faulty gene. This may be inherited or crop up as a result of mutation when **DNA** is copied within the **cells** of the body. In other cases, there are many genes involved in a single genetic condition. These are known as multi-gene disorders. Other health conditions, such as an illness early in life, or the **environment** where a person grows up, can also interact with the abnormal genes. So, some people with the abnormal genes suffer problems while others do not. Examples of conditions with these more complex causes, involving many genes and also the environment, include allergies and asthma. The medical phrase for such conditions is that they have 'inherited components'. Most people would say that the conditions 'run in families'.

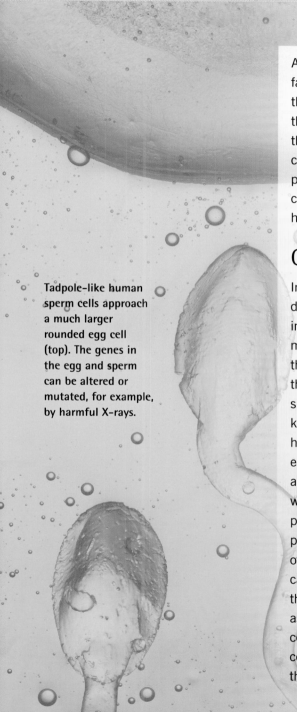

Tadpole-like human sperm cells approach a much larger rounded egg cell (top). The genes in the egg and sperm can be altered or mutated, for example, by harmful X-rays.

# Treating genetic conditions

In the womb, a baby's umbilical cord joins to the mother and brings oxygen and nutrients. If the baby has any genetic problems, the cord could also provide stem cells for treatment.

**❝Stem cells are one of the most fascinating areas of biology today. But like many expanding fields of scientific inquiry, research on stem cells raises scientific questions as rapidly as it generates new discoveries.❞**

US National Institutes of Health Stem Cell Information Report, 2003

There are many different treatments for genetic conditions, depending on the individual case. They include medical drugs and products, such as clotting factor for haemophilia (see page 19). There are also surgical operations to correct conditions such as spina bifida and cleft palate. In cleft palate the upper lip, roof of the mouth and lower nose do not form properly and have a cleft or gap. These types of treatments are often very successful.

## GE as a cure

Some genetic conditions which cause long-term problems may become treatable by **genetic engineering**. Examples include cystic fibrosis and immunodeficiency syndrome (where the body cannot fight against invading germs effectively). The aim is to alter the **genes** themselves within the body, so that they work normally again; this is known as gene therapy. This would, in effect, cure the problem rather than just treat the symptoms.

Various forms of gene therapy are being tested. In one method, normal versions of the genes are introduced into the body, to replace the genes that are faulty. The normal genes may be wrapped up within, or attached to, substances that are naturally taken into **cells**. The aim is that these new genes will add themselves into the existing genetic material.

## Stem cells

Another method is to replace whole cells that have the faulty genes, with new cells that have normal genes. These cells can come from a number of sources – for example, from another person, as when someone donates a kidney or bone marrow for transplant. Another method is to use **stem cells**. These are 'general' cells, which have not yet become specialized into nerve cells, muscle cells or other cells with specific shapes and roles. Sources of stem cells include the patient's own body, the umbilical cord which links an unborn baby to its mother in the womb and human embryos – human bodies in the very early stages of development.

Overall progress in gene therapies as practical treatments is very slow. In one set of tests, far from being cured, two of the patients being treated for immunodeficiency developed the serious condition of leukaemia. There are also great debates about using genetic material from sources such as embryos, as described on page 42.

# Biotechnology

One of the major uses of **biotechnology** is to make medical products such as **antibiotics** and other drugs, and **hormones** such as **insulin** (see page 19). One of the most successful is growth hormone, as described opposite. Newer bioengineered products include some vaccines used for immunizations, which protect the body against infectious diseases.

Several projects around the world aim to put **genes** for making vaccines into foods, so that the vaccine can be grown and eaten rather than manufactured and injected. Tests have been carried out on potatoes that contain an edible vaccine against the disease hepatitis B. This affects the liver and causes many health problems around the body. Many experts believe that one of the best foods for this task could be the banana. It is readily available and comes in its own wrapping of skin, so it is germ-free when peeled. It needs no cooking or processing, it is easy to eat – and most people like bananas!

One day, instead of needing vaccinations, eating a GM banana could protect the body against diseases such as measles, mumps and rubella.

## Foods and fuels

Bioengineered microbes are now being used to produce many food products. People who follow a vegan diet usually avoid all animal substances, including animal-based cheeses. Even some plant-based 'vegetarian' cheeses are processed using substances obtained from cattle. GE microbes can now produce substitutes for these, to make wholly non-animal vegan cheeses.

Another group of products which could be made by GM plants is biofuels, based on plant oils like canola (oilseed rape) or sunflower. These would be burned in car engines or power stations as less polluting, more **sustainable** alternatives to petrol and oil. Further examples include new pesticides, and chemicals that can break up or disperse oils, for example, in a slick spilled on to the sea or in contaminated soil.

## Case study  Growing well

In the body, growth hormone controls growth from infancy to adulthood. In some children this hormone is lacking and growth is slow. Formerly, growth hormone was taken from the bodies of people who had recently died. This was complicated and expensive. From 1985, human growth hormone was made by bioengineered microbes. Many more children could receive it and grow normally. In developed countries about one child in 10,000 now receives growth hormone treatment.

# Cloning

Clones are living things with exactly the same **genes** as each other. They exist naturally in various forms. Some simple animals like worms reproduce by simply dividing their bodies into parts, which grow into new individuals with the same genes as the 'parent'. In animals or people, identical twins come from the same original single **cell**, the fertilized egg, and so they have the same genes.

## Making clones

Clones can also be created by modern **genetic engineering**. A set of genetic material is obtained from the cell of a **donor** living thing, such as a plant or animal. This genetic material or **DNA** is put into an egg cell, which has had its own genetic material removed. The egg cell is stimulated to start multiplying by adding certain chemicals or giving it a tiny electric shock. It develops into a new individual with the same genes as the original donor, so the two are clones.

## Why clone?

Many thousands of plants have been cloned by traditional gardening methods such as cuttings and graftings. Dozens of creatures have now been cloned by modern genetic methods, including farm animals such as cows, sheep and pigs. The idea is to choose an animal with a desired feature and copy it. For example, a cow that yields the greatest amount of milk could be cloned so that all the cows in the herd are champion milkers. It has been suggested that extremely rare animals or plants could be cloned to help save them from extinction. Cloning and other genetic engineering methods could even be applied to genetic material from the remains of extinct species, to 'bring them back to life'.

Woolly mammoths are extinct – they have all died out. But could DNA obtained from their deep-frozen bodies, occasionally found in ice, be used to bring them back to life again?

# Cloning problems

Clones may have the same genes, but they are never identical copies. As described earlier, the development of a living thing is affected by its **environment** and life events as well as by genes. So, a herd of cows cloned from a champion milker may well grow up differently and not all give plentiful milk. Also, if a serious disease strikes, then the natural genetic variation in a normal cow herd may mean that some animals are more resistant to the disease and survive. In a cloned herd with no genetic variety, they may all die.

Dolly was the first mammal cloned from the body cells of another adult mammal, rather than from embryo cells. She is shown here with her lamb Bonnie. Dolly suffered joint problems and died in 2003.

# Health risks to people

The science of **genetic engineering** is very new and very complicated. Genetic experts advise that in addition to the challenges and problems faced today, there will be questions to ask and problems to solve in the future, which we cannot even imagine as yet. Also, scientific tests and safety studies take time. So the various effects of genetic engineering and GM products on people's health and well-being will take many years to assess.

## How might risks arise?

At this early stage in the development of genetic engineering, both as a science and a useful technology, how might GM products affect human health? There are many suggested ways, both direct and indirect. Direct problems could result from eating GM crops or GM animal products, with harm to the body's digestive system or other parts.

Another risk might be consuming animals, whether GM or not, which have themselves eaten GM products such as bioengineered crops. In this example GM products enter the 'food chain', which is the series of events where a plant is eaten by an animal, which is then eaten by another animal, or perhaps by a person. The effects of GM organisms on food chains in plants and animals could disrupt the balance of nature and affect **ecosystems**. For example, a GM crop might be eaten by caterpillars, which die as a result. This in turn affects birds that rely on catching the caterpillars at breeding time, to feed to their chicks. If humans are involved in the food chain, we could also be affected.

## Further risks

Genetically engineering living things might cause other health problems. Bioengineered microbes could suddenly become powerful germs or 'superbugs' and cause new kinds of infectious diseases. This could happen not only in people, but in animals such as farm livestock, and maybe in plants such as farm crops. If a new GM-caused disease devastated rice crops, then half the people in the world might starve.

There are many questions about whether these kinds of GM-caused disasters will happen in the future. The only answer we have for the present is: 'We don't yet know.'

> **"**Many millions of people, particularly in the United States, Canada and Argentina, have for seven years been eating food products derived from animals fed on GM diets and no substantiated ill effects have been reported.**"**
>
> First report of the UK's GM Science Review, July 2003

The effects on our health of most traditional crops are known. New GM crops could provide more food, but their health effects might take years to assess.

# Types of health problems

There are many possible ways in which GM products could cause health problems in people. Particles or dust from GM plants or animals could be breathed into the airways and lungs, and cause damage in the way that tobacco smoke causes lung **cancer**. Another suggestion is that a GM product could affect the skin by contact, producing a rash or itchy spots, either by chemical irritation or an allergic reaction. A food allergy to a GM product could cause similar symptoms in the skin, as well as swelling of body parts and other problems. Another concern is that GM material might be taken from the digested food in the intestines, into the human body. Here it could cause illness, including forms of cancer.

## Evidence either way

There are reported individual cases of people who feel ill after encountering GM products. But there are no long-term or large scientific studies which show that GM products definitely cause illness in people. There are also no similar studies showing GM products are totally safe. The UK's GM Science Review of July 2003 reports that current possible risks to human health are 'very low'. It also points out the need to carry out extensive scientific tests. It advises that, at present, there can be no overall decision about GM's uses being harmful or harmless. It is necessary to treat each GM product on its own merits and as a separate case.

The airways and linings deep in the lungs are very delicate and prone to damage caused by bacterial germs (green). Breathing in dust particles from GM products could also harm the delicate lung linings.

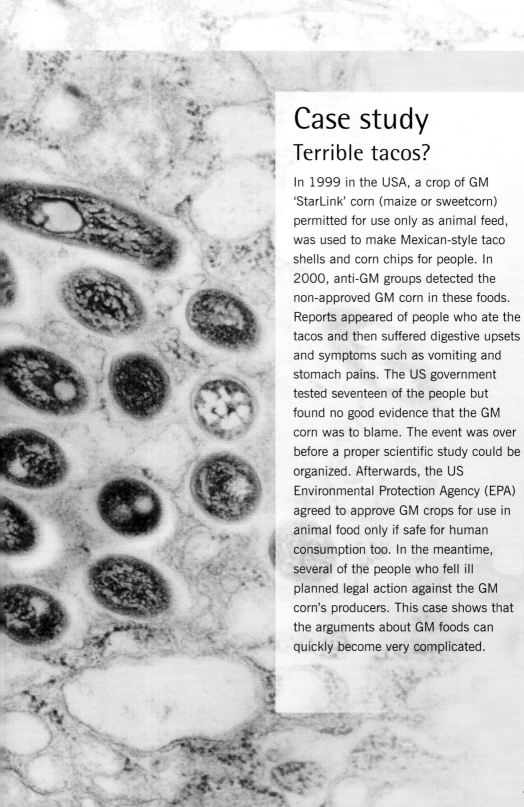

# Case study
## Terrible tacos?

In 1999 in the USA, a crop of GM 'StarLink' corn (maize or sweetcorn) permitted for use only as animal feed, was used to make Mexican-style taco shells and corn chips for people. In 2000, anti-GM groups detected the non-approved GM corn in these foods. Reports appeared of people who ate the tacos and then suffered digestive upsets and symptoms such as vomiting and stomach pains. The US government tested seventeen of the people but found no good evidence that the GM corn was to blame. The event was over before a proper scientific study could be organized. Afterwards, the US Environmental Protection Agency (EPA) agreed to approve GM crops for use in animal food only if safe for human consumption too. In the meantime, several of the people who fell ill planned legal action against the GM corn's producers. This case shows that the arguments about GM foods can quickly become very complicated.

# Risks to the environment

Apart from the risks to human health, what are the risks posed by various GM products to the well-being of our surroundings or **environment** and our wildlife? One concern is the possibility of **gene flow** or 'genetic contamination'. This is the movement of new or novel **genes** from where they are supposed to be, in GM living things, into other kinds of living things where they might cause great problems.

Some anti-GM campaigns highlight the danger of genes 'escaping' like this. Suppose a gene which gives resistance to a certain herbicide chemical is put into a GM crop. But then somehow, an insect does what genetic engineers do – transfers the gene to another species. This happens in nature, although rarely. However, with genes already transferred once, the risk of a second transfer might be higher. This is an example of how little we know about GM organisms. The insect could suck in sap from the GM crop, then do the same to a weed, but 'inject' some of the resistant genes. Or a GM plant's pollen (male breeding **cells**) might spread unexpectedly far and contaminate or crossbreed with weeds elsewhere. Again, this happens rarely in nature, but the risks of it occurring with new gene combinations are unknown. The result could be a 'superweed' that resists herbicide sprays, and spreads to smother crops across vast regions. Similar events could happen with insects and other animals, leading to plagues of 'superpests' that devastate not only farm crops but wild plants too. This could reduce the food for wild animals and affect food chains and the balance of nature. Another problem is that the weedkillers sprayed on GM crops could put at risk many insects, birds and other animals, who depend on

Birds like the yellowhammer thrive on the flowers and seeds of weed plants. Weedkillers used for GM crops could be more effective at removing weeds and so reduce the birds' food supply.

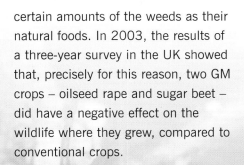

certain amounts of the weeds as their natural foods. In 2003, the results of a three-year survey in the UK showed that, precisely for this reason, two GM crops – oilseed rape and sugar beet – did have a negative effect on the wildlife where they grew, compared to conventional crops.

## For and against

There is very little scientific evidence either for or against these types of possibilities. Some GM supporters say that if extensive tests and studies show no problems with GM crops or animals, then permission should be given for their use. An anti-GM view is that somehow, one day, gene transfer might occur in ways we cannot know, and cause terrible problems. Then, once the gene has 'escaped' into wild animals or plants, it cannot be recaptured. So it is better to ban GM and avoid the risk.

**❝The risk is so small that it is almost not even there, almost impossible to measure.❞**

Professor Markham Sears, Department of Environmental Biology, University of Guelph, Canada, in September 2001. He was speaking about two-year research projects, which showed that the pollen of GM corn (maize) did not cause large-scale harm to the caterpillars of monarch butterflies, as previous reports had claimed.

Some scientific studies are checking the effects of GM crops on wildlife such as monarch butterfly caterpillars. Early reports said the caterpillars were harmed, but later reports said they were probably not.

# Does GE make the rich richer?

There is great debate about the business side of **genetic engineering**, especially in the production of GM crops and medicines. Some people fear that genetic engineering and **biotechnology** companies will force farmers, patients and other consumers to buy their products at increased prices.

## Sneaky business?

One suggestion or scenario is that a farmer begins to grow a GM crop that

International agreements try to reduce the price of drugs used to treat terrible diseases, such as HIV/AIDS. GM medicines could help this process and allow poorer countries to fight disease epidemics more effectively.

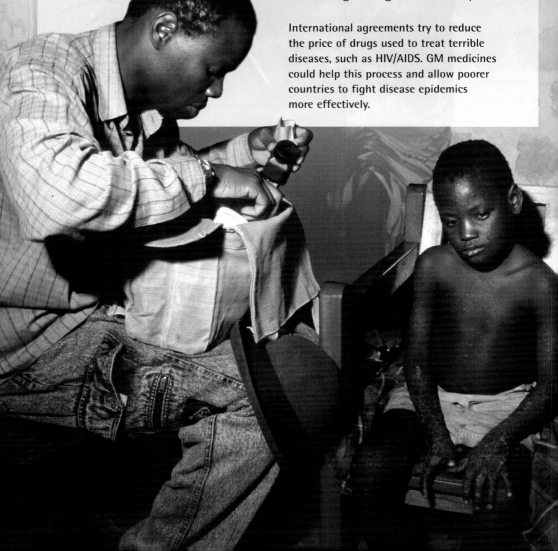

has been made resistant to a certain herbicide. The farmer buys the crop seeds from the manufacturer, which happens to be a powerful international company. The herbicide, to which the crop is resistant, is made by the same company. So, the farmer has to buy this too. At first, the farmer's profits rise. But then the manufacturer increases the price of the seeds. This reduces income for the farmer but gives the manufacturer more profit. The manufacturer tries to 'help' by offering the farmer seed supplies for the next five years at a slightly reduced price. But next year, the price of the herbicide goes up. Again, the farmer's profits fall while those of the manufacturer rise.

Since many genetic engineering and biotechnology companies are based in developed countries, and sell their seeds to developing countries, this means the rich get richer at the expense of the poor. Five corporations dominate the development of GM, and one of these produced over three-quarters of GM crops grown commercially around the world during the early 2000s.

Similar arguments are proposed for the possible sale of GM-produced medical drugs, such as those which combat **AIDS**, the condition caused by **HIV**. However, international pressure produced agreements in 2002–3. Several major drug companies reduced the cost of their anti-AIDS drugs when sold to developing nations, especially in Africa. Similar discussions are taking place about projects to develop drugs against other conditions, such as hepatitis and malaria.

## The power of big business

Around the world, tests and experiments with **genes** are being carried out by thousands of small companies, academic organizations like universities, and government laboratories. However, making a potential GM product such as a new drug or crop into a commercial success takes vast amounts of money – usually hundreds of millions of dollars. Only big biotech companies have these amounts of money. So they 'buy up' potential new GM products, and like many other kinds of big business around the world, become even more powerful.

# Can GE/GM feed and cure the world?

Can the genetic revolution help to raise food production levels, reduce famine, provide drugs to treat major illnesses and generally improve life for people around the world? Of course, it is still far too early to know, but not too soon to start the debate.

## Positive aims

GM supporters point out that the general aims of genetic technologies are positive, such as to improve farm crops and animals, manufacture drugs and medicines more effectively and cure genetic conditions. For example, crops could be made that are resistant to major

Another crop harvest fails in the dry lands of Ethiopia. Supporters of GM say that one day drought-resistant crops could grow well in these regions.

insect pests, such as worms and grubs. Currently these pests can devastate whole fields, especially in poorer areas where farmers cannot afford to spray them with pesticide chemicals. 'Golden Rice' (see below) and various other crops are being engineered to provide extra vitamins for improving the health of millions.

## More out, but more in

Some GM crop trials have shown increased yields per hectare, compared to non-GM crops, in places as far apart as Canada, Mexico, Israel, India, China and Australia. But in many of these cases, the extra 'output', in the form of products for sale, was helped by extra 'input', too. This was in the form of more fertilizers and nutrients, increased spraying of herbicides and pesticides and other methods of crop care. Overall, there are few examples of GM increasing the total efficiency of farming. Yet increased efficiency is a major aim of many GM crop projects, especially those intended for poorer regions.

Many people argue that plant breeding by traditional methods, selecting different varieties to reproduce together, could bring similar benefits. The methods are slower, but tried and tested, and could cost far less than GM. Using traditional techniques, crops could be developed to grow on salty soils or in drought-prone areas, or to contain extra nutrients, without the possible risks linked to GM methods.

# Case study
## Ups and downs of 'Golden Rice'

'Golden Rice' is a GM version of rice altered to provide the body with extra vitamins. Lack of vitamins in the diet can cause a variety of illnesses. Lack of vitamin A, for example, causes blindness and death in millions of people in poorer countries. But the international effort to produce 'Golden Rice' has hit many problems. Tests of the crops have been disappointing. Larger-scale test growing has been delayed several times, and may be put off for years. Many experts believe the well-intentioned project faces a bleak future.

# Should we create or own life?

For some people, the main worries about **genetic engineering** are not so much the possible harm to people or the **environment**. Their debate concerns genetic engineering's central aim: to make new forms of life. Many people hold ethical or moral views, or follow religions or faiths, which do not allow them to support genetic research, or use GM products, or receive genetic medical treatment – even if their lives are at risk. They believe forms of life should be created naturally, or by the gods or deities they believe in, and not by people in laboratories for commercial gain.

## Cells or beings?

The areas of genetic medicine and **gene** therapy can be especially difficult. An active area of research is the use of **stem cells** to treat or cure genetic conditions. One source of stem cells is an early human embryo. This is a tiny ball of **microscopic** cells smaller than the dot on this 'i', long before any recognizable body parts such as the brain or heart develop. However, for some people, the embryo is seen as a new human life which should not be disturbed or harmed by taking away its cells for genetic research.

## Patenting new life

As a company develops a new invention, like a faster microchip for computers, it usually has to spend huge amounts of money. The company is then granted a patent for the invention.

Research on very early embryos of living things, like this microscopic speck of cells, can help progress in genetic engineering. But should such work be allowed?

This prevents other people from taking advantage by copying and selling it for their own profit. Businesses and industries say that patents are vital. They allow a company to earn back the money it spent in developing the product and also fund new research.

Should the patent system apply to genetic engineering? It does already. Gene companies have some 1000 patents on individual genes, new combinations of genes and whole GM organisms. They say that patents allow them to finance their past work and future research.

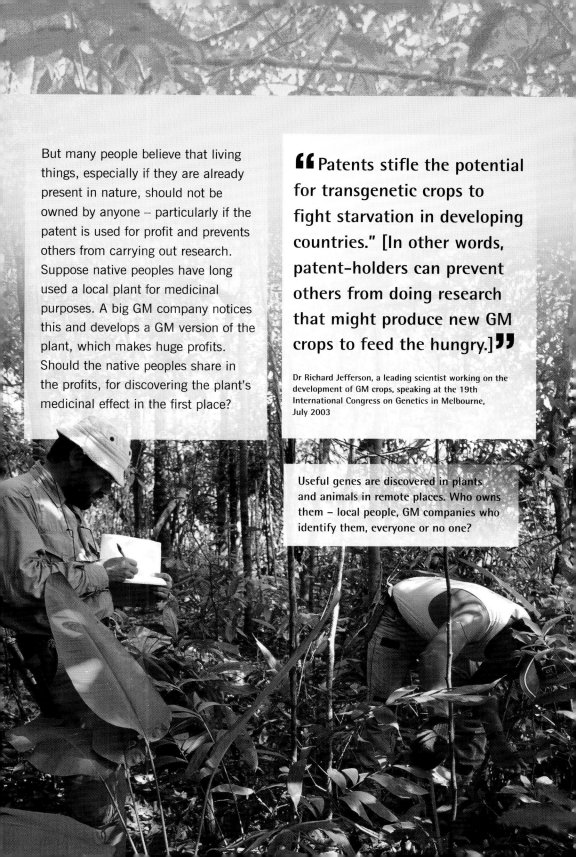

But many people believe that living things, especially if they are already present in nature, should not be owned by anyone – particularly if the patent is used for profit and prevents others from carrying out research. Suppose native peoples have long used a local plant for medicinal purposes. A big GM company notices this and develops a GM version of the plant, which makes huge profits. Should the native peoples share in the profits, for discovering the plant's medicinal effect in the first place?

**❝Patents stifle the potential for transgenetic crops to fight starvation in developing countries." [In other words, patent-holders can prevent others from doing research that might produce new GM crops to feed the hungry.]❞**

Dr Richard Jefferson, a leading scientist working on the development of GM crops, speaking at the 19th International Congress on Genetics in Melbourne, July 2003

Useful genes are discovered in plants and animals in remote places. Who owns them – local people, GM companies who identify them, everyone or no one?

# Controls, tests and trials

The process of developing and testing a new GM organism or product is lengthy and costly. It is estimated that at least 100 new GM crops must be produced, to find just one which might then be developed for commercial success. During this development the chances of failure are still high. With animals, the difficulties are even greater. Perhaps 500 new GM versions will yield only one possible success. With GM drugs and medicines, the numbers and chances of failure are greater still.

## Endless tests

At each stage, the GM organism or product is tested for possibly harmful effects on people, animals, plants and the **environment**. For example, a GM food is checked to see if it might cause an allergic reaction. Supporters of **genetic engineering** say that all these tests and trials ensure that GM foods are as safe as possible. In fact, they point out that similar foods produced by the traditional methods of **selective breeding** do not have to undergo

Early tests on GM crops are carried out in tents or greenhouses, to lessen the chance of their pollen and seeds spreading into the wild.

## Who grows GM crops?

Around the world, four countries grow almost all of GM crops produced on a commercial scale. They are the USA, with the vast majority (66 per cent ) of all the crops, then Argentina (23 per cent), Canada and China. The main GM crops are soya, maize (corn) and cotton, which together account for 95 per cent of all commercial GM planting. Other crops include canola (oilseed rape), squash, potato, papaya, sunflower and sugarbeet.

these types of tests at all. But anti-GM campaigners suggest that no amount of testing can prove that a product is safe. There are examples of crops and drugs produced by traditional non-GM methods, which were tested thoroughly at the time, but problems then came to light many years later. One example was the drug thalidomide, which was used to treat feelings of sickness in pregnant women. But after some years' use it was found to cause malformations in their babies, such as missing or mis-shaped limbs. It was rapidly withdrawn.

## Varying standards

However, in regions around the world, scientific work is carried out to varying standards and regulations. The world's most populous nation, China, has approved more GM plant products than any other country. In most cases, these have been developed by scientists working for the Chinese government. But access to their work is often difficult for scientists from other nations, who might wish to study the methods and check the results.

# What people know – or think they know

Opinion polls in many countries show that people are aware of **genetic engineering**, and especially of GM foods and products. But these surveys also show that, in general, genetic issues do not come very high on most people's lists of concerns. Topics such as employment, education and the level of crime feature much more strongly. Anti-GM campaigners are sometimes criticized for saying that genetic issues concern people greatly, when this is not really the case.

These surveys also show that public opinion varies around the world. The USA produces most GM foods. There are no requirements here for labels or packages to say if the foods or their ingredients are GM. Also, people have been eating such foods since 1996 without clear and large-scale examples of harm. For many US citizens genetic engineering and GM products, and their possible risks to human health, wildlife and the **environment,** are very small worries. In China, where many people produce their own foods, labelling is a very minor concern indeed.

## Greater concerns

In the European Union, GM foods or ingredients must be labelled if they contain more than 1 per cent of GM product, but not otherwise. EU citizens are more aware than those in the USA of the possible risks to health and the environment. They want to see GM foods labelled, so that they can make consumer choices. In the UK most major food retailers, including large supermarkets, promote the information that they sell no, or very few, GM foods or products.

In New Zealand, the food labelling requirements are similar to those in the EU. New Zealand had banned commercial development of all GM organisms and products. But the ban was lifted in 2003, because of fears that New Zealand would fall behind and lose out to others that were already producing GM crops, drugs and other products. These examples show the huge range of official laws and regulations around the world, and how public attitudes and opinions. differ from one region to another.

## Soil to shelf

Labelling foods with GM ingredients, especially for processed foods like ready-made meals, can cause enormous problems. It means knowing where all the ingredients came from, and whether they are GM or not. In turn this means huge amounts of tracking or tracing batches of GM crops and animals. If different countries have different rules, labels and packaging have to be produced separately for each of them. Such extra work and record-keeping at all stages, from 'soil to shelf', could push up the price of food.

Many consumers will distrust genetic engineering and prefer non-GM products, perhaps until GM products have been tried and tested over many years.

**❝The lessons of history tell us that sometimes we have rushed forward incautiously to exploit new technologies, only subsequently to appreciate the medical, social, environmental and other costs.❞**

First report of the UK's Science Review, July 2003

# What can you do?

Experts on genetic issues, such as **cloning** and GM foods, often say that there are three main attitudes among the general public. Some want GE/GM, some don't, and some don't care either way. If you feel strongly about such issues, and perhaps want to find out more, or wish to campaign, there are many different sources of information you can access. These include books, magazines and newspaper columns. Websites also carry information. But the nature of the Internet means that some of their facts are less than accurate.

## Campaigns

As shown on page 52, there are numerous groups to join, especially those wanting to ban or lessen genetic research and GM products, or to introduce greater controls. Actions include signing petitions, attending campaign marches and contacting large **biotechnology** companies, public officials such as councillors and government members, and other influential people.

Marches and demonstrations are ways of campaigning – either in support of GM products or, as here, against them.

48

Consumer pressure can often bring much publicity. Some people support the idea of bans or boycotts on certain products or manufacturers. Others set up demonstrations with placards and posters in public places, such as outside large stores or in town squares.

## Special interests

Some people focus on areas of particular interest. These might include the risk that GM crops could contaminate other living things and spread damaging **genes** into the food chain and **environment**. Another area of great public interest is medical research on **stem cells** and cloning. These are complex topics. Many people find that their opinions change as they discover more information and come to understand the issues more fully. Some change from supporting GM to being anti-GM, while others do the opposite.

For example, some people are against any kind of cloning of human **cells** and tissues. They might imagine super-armies cloned from the best soldiers, which could take over the world!

However, suppose that stem cells could be taken at the birth of each baby, from its umbilical cord (which is usually disposed of in any case), and stored. If that baby grew up and fell ill later, it might be possible to clone the cells and grow them into a new body part, to replace the diseased one and so cure the illness.

These types of possibilities can change a person's views, especially when they have close links with what is happening in that person's life. People who were previously healthy and anti-GM may change their opinions if they become ill – and only GM-based medicines could save their lives.

**❝Genes belong on legs, not in food, they make it too chewy.❞**

Billy Connolly, comedian, as part of his stand-up routine, 2000

**49**

# Facts and figures

## Main GM crops

Worldwide, the four main GM crops grown commercially are:

| | |
|---|---|
| Soybean | 62 per cent |
| Maize (corn/sweetcorn) | 21 per cent |
| Cotton | 12 per cent |
| Canola (oilseed rape) | 3 per cent |

Other GM crops such as potatoes, tomatoes and tobacco are
grown in small amounts.

## Total worldwide GM crop coverage

In 2002, coverage was almost 60 million hectares (over twice the area of the UK).

## Proportion of GM crop area by nation

| | |
|---|---|
| USA | 66 per cent |
| Argentina | 23 per cent |
| Canada | 6 per cent |
| China | 4 per cent |

Other nations growing GM crops commercially include Australia, Bulgaria,
Colombia, Germany, Honduras, India, Indonesia, Mexico, Romania, South Africa,
Spain and Uruguay. In total, between 6 and 7 million farmers grow GM crops, and
three-quarters of them are from poorer or developing nations.

## Reasons why GM crops are grown

| | |
|---|---|
| Resistance or tolerance to herbicides | 75 per cent |
| Resistance to insect pests | 15 per cent |
| Both of the above | 7 per cent |
| Other features, such as larger yield per plant | 3 per cent |

Source: GM Science Review, July 2003

# Cloned animals

More than 150 animals have been **cloned**, some with their natural **genes** and some after genetic modification. The various reasons include:

Sheep – wool, meat, milk containing valuable products such as medicinal drugs
Cows – altered milk, meat
Pigs – organs and 'spare parts' to transplant into humans
Horses – research into breeding thoroughbred racehorses
Mules – clone of a champion racer
Mice and rats – as laboratory test animals
Rhesus monkeys – for scientific tests on inherited diseases
Cats – perhaps to 'continue the life' of a much-loved family pet
Salmon – faster, more efficient growth

# Genomes

Complete or almost complete **genome** sequences, for the order of the sub-units or **bases** in the **DNA**, are known for more than 200 living things, including microbes, fungi, plants and animals. Examples include:

More than 150 microbes including bacteria and yeasts (fungi), some harmful and some useful.

Single-celled alga *Guillardia theta* (simple plant)

Mouse-ear cress *Arabidopsis thaliana* (small flowering plant)

Rice *Oryza sativa*

Roundworm *Caenorhabditis* (tiny nematode worm)

Fruit-fly *Drosophila melanogaster*

Zebrafish *Danio rerio* (tropical fish)

Rat (laboratory)

Mouse (laboratory)

Human being

# Human genetic diseases

Worldwide, one baby in 30 is born with an inherited or **congenital** disorder. Severe disorders, causing early death or life-long health problems, occur in about one child in 70 in developed countries, and one child in 25 in some less developed regions.

# Further information

## Contacts in the UK

**Genetic Interest Group (GIG)**
Unit 4d, Leroy House,
436 Essex Road,
London N1 3QP
Tel: 020 7704 3141
**www.gig.org.uk**

A national alliance of organizations with a membership of over 120 charities, which supports children, families and individuals affected by genetic disorders. GIG also provides information on new discoveries and treatments, and generally promotes awareness and understanding of genetic disorders so that high quality services for people affected by genetic conditions are made available to all who need them.

**Human Genetics Alert / Campaign Against Human Genetic Engineering**
PO Box 6313,
London N16 0DY
Tel: 020 8809 4513
email: cahge@globalnet.co.uk
**www.hgalert.org**
**www.users.globalnet.co.uk/~cahge**

HGA is an international and independent public interest watchdog group based in London, committed to informing people about human genetics issues, and to putting forward clear policies that serve the public interest.

**Compassion in World Farming**
Charles House,
5A Charles Street,
Petersfield,
Hampshire GU32 3EH
Tel: 01730 264208 / 268863
email: compassion@ciwf.co.uk
**www.ciwf.co.uk**

Campaigning to improve the welfare of farmed animals through peaceful protest and lobbying, including issues raised by genetic engineering (see **www.ciwf.co.uk/Camp/Main/Genetic/genetic_campaign.htm**).

**Roslin Institute**
Roslin BioCentre,
Midlothian EH25 9PS
Scotland
Tel: 0131 527 4200
**www.roslin.ac.uk**

One of the world's leading scientific institutes with a wide range of disciplines including molecular and cell biology, quantitative genetics, endocrinology, developmental biology, animal behaviour and nutrition, especially applied to farm and laboratory animal species. This is where Dolly the sheep was produced. Roslin takes a keen interest in the public discussions related to genetics work (see, for example, the website area **www.roslin.ac.uk/public/cloning.html**).

**Food Standards Agency (FSA)**
Aviation House,
125 Kingsway,
London WC2B 6NH
Tel: 020 7276 8000
**www.foodstandards.gov.uk**

The UK's independent food safety watchdog set up by an Act of Parliament in 2000 to protect the public's health and consumer interests in relation to food. On GM labelling, the FSA supports consumer choice and recognizes that some people may choose not to buy or not to eat GM foods however carefully they have been assessed for safety. (For labelling matters see their website area **www.foodstandards.gov.uk/foodlabelling**.)

**Human Genome Organization (HUGO)**
International Office,
HUGO,
144 Harley Street,
London W1G 7LD
Tel: 020 7935 8085
email: hugo@hugo-international.org
**www.gene.ucl.ac.uk/hugo/**

HUGO's mission is to promote international discussion and collaboration on the worldwide human genome initiative, to analyse the human genome as rapidly and effectively as possible, to promote the scientific study of the human genome, and to encourage the free flow of information about the genome. HUGO also provides a forum for addressing the scientific, medical, ethical, legal, social and commercial issues raised by genome knowledge.

**Human Fertilisation and Embryology Authority (HFEA)**
Paxton House,
30 Artillery Lane,
London E1 7LS
Tel: 020 7377 5077
email: admin@hfea.gov.uk
**www.hfea.gov.uk**

A non-departmental UK government body that regulates and inspects all UK clinics providing IVF or 'test tube baby' services, donor sperm insemination or the storage of eggs, sperm or embryos. The HFEA also licenses and monitors the human embryo research being planned or conducted in the UK.

# Contact in the USA

**The Campaign to Label Genetically Engineered Foods**
The Campaign,
PO Box 55699,
Seattle, WA 98155
Tel: +1 425-771-4049
email: label@thecampaign.org
**www.thecampaign.org**

A US-based campaign that offers news updates, educational information and ways to lobby for clearer, more accurate labels on GM foods and similar products. It is active both in the USA and around the world.

# Contacts in Australia and New Zealand

**Food Standards Australia New Zealand**
*In Australia:*
Boeing House
55 Blackall Street
Barton, ACT 2600
Australia
Tel: +61 2 6271 2222
Email: info@foodstandards.gov.au
**www.foodstandards.gov.au/**

*In New Zealand:*
108 The Terrace
Wellington
New Zealand
Tel: +64 4 473 9942
Email: info@foodstandards.govt.nz
**www.foodstandards.gov.au/**
GM web pages include:
**www.foodstandards.gov.au/whatsinfood/gmfoods/index.cfm**

FSANZ ensures safe food by developing food standards with advice from other government agencies, input from stakeholders and food regulatory policies endorsed by the Australia and New Zealand Food Regulation Ministerial Council. FSANZ is involved in regulation, labelling, safety and provision of factsheets.

# Further reading

*The Debate over Human Cloning: A Pro/Con Issue*, David Goodnough (Enslow Publishers, Inc., 2003)

*Genetic Engineering: Debating the Benefits and Concerns* (Issues in Focus series), Karen Judson (Enslow Publishers, Inc., 2001)

*The Debate over Genetically Engineered Foods: Healthy or Harmful?* (Issues in Focus series), Kathiann M. Kowalski (Enslow Publishers, Inc., 2002)

*Cloning*, Daniel Cohen (Illustrator) (Millbrook Press, 2002)

*DNA and Genetic Engineering* (Cells & Life series), Robert Snedden (Heinemann Library, 2003)

*Genetic Engineering* (Current Controversies series), Lisa Yount (Editor) (Greenhaven Press, 2002)

# Glossary

## AIDS
Acquired Immune Deficiency Syndrome, a condition that reduces the body's defences against germs and disease. It is caused by the microbe HIV (see below).

## antibiotic
drug that acts against germs (harmful microbes), usually the kinds called bacteria

## bacteria
types of single-celled microbes found almost everywhere in the world. Some are harmful, causing infectious diseases.

## bases
in the genetic material DNA (see below), the parts or sub-units which form the rungs of the DNA ladder and which contain the genetic information as a chemical code

## biotechnology
use of living things, especially microbes like bacteria, as tiny 'factories' to make products such as useful chemicals, usually by altering their genetic material

## cancers
forms of disease in which some of the microscopic cells in the body go out of control and multiply abnormally and rapidly, for example, forming a growth or tumour

## cells
microscopic building-blocks of life, on average one-fortieth of 1 millimetre across

## chromosomes
thread-like lengths of genetic material, DNA, carrying many genes

## clones
living things which have exactly the same genes as each other

## congenital
describes a medical condition, illness or similar problem that is present at birth

## DNA
de-oxyribonucleic acid, the chemical substance which contains information in the form of genes (see below)

## donor
person who donates, which in medicine usually means giving part of the body such as blood, a kidney or bone marrow

## double helix
the shape of DNA, which is two long strands lying side by side and twisted or coiled into a helix (like two corkscrews)

## ecosystem
all living things in a particular place, which can be small like a pond or huge like the ocean. In particular, how these living things interact with each other and with their surroundings or environment.

## environment
everything in the surroundings, including living and non-living things

## gene flow
when genes spread or move, usually as living things breeding with each other, so that their genes are passed to their offspring in new places

## genes
instructions for how a living thing develops, grows and carries out life processes, in the form of the chemical DNA

## genetic engineering
altering genes or genetic material, usually by processes in the laboratory

**genetics**
the study of genes, how they work, and how they pass during reproduction (breeding) from one generation to the next

**genome**
all of the genes in a particular living thing

**HIV**
Human Immunodeficiency Virus, which causes AIDS (see above)

**hormone**
natural chemical in a living thing that controls a process in its body, such as growth, the use of energy or reproduction

**inherit**
to receive genes from parents. Also, to have a bodily feature, such as eye colour, which is controlled by genes passed from parents.

**insulin**
hormone (see above) that controls the use of the body's main energy source, glucose or blood sugar

**interferon**
medical drug that treats some forms of cancer and attacks or disables certain kinds of viruses

**microscopic**
too small to see in detail, unless looking through a microscope – generally an object which is less than about one-tenth of 1 millimetre across

**mutations**
changes in genes

**nanometre**
very tiny unit of length – one nanometre is one-millionth of 1 millimetre

**nucleus**
the control centre of a cell, usually containing the genetic material DNA

**phages**
particular types of the tiniest microbes, viruses, which attack and get inside bacteria

**radiation**
rays or waves of energy that are a combination of electricity and magnetism

**recipient cells**
living cells that receive new genes, in the form of the genetic material DNA

**recombination**
when genes are put together or shuffled in new combinations or assortments, not usually found in nature

**restriction enzymes**
different types of chemicals, each breaking or cutting a length of DNA at a certain place

**selective breeding**
when living things are chosen by people to breed together, to produce new, desired combinations of features

**stem cells**
cells at the early stage of development, which are generalized and not yet specialized to do a particular task

**sustainable**
describes a process that can continue for a long time, without running out of raw materials, energy and other needs

# Index